My Room

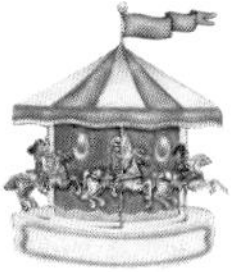

Beryl Smith

Illustrated by Rick Faust

Dominie Press, Inc.

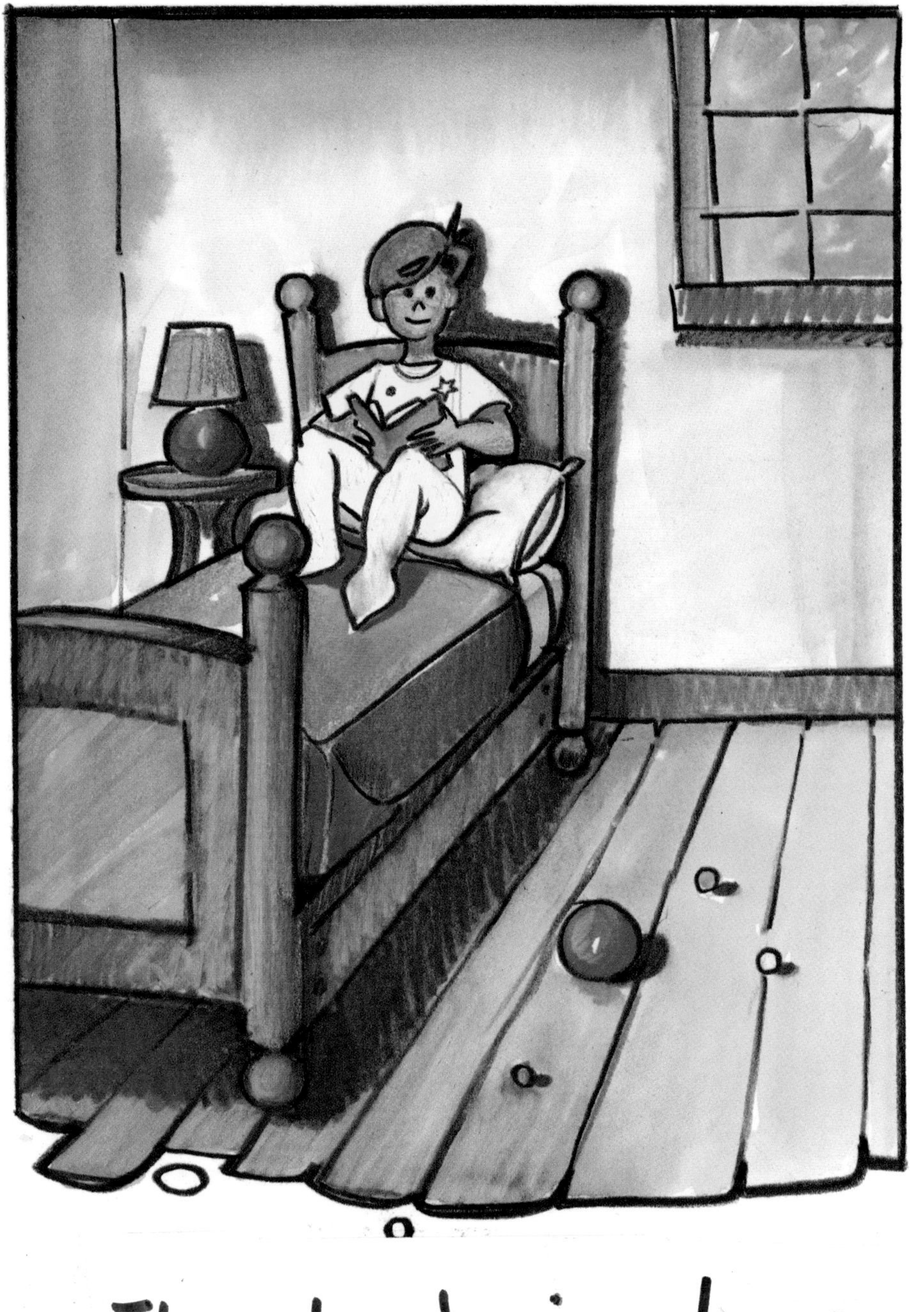

The bed is here.

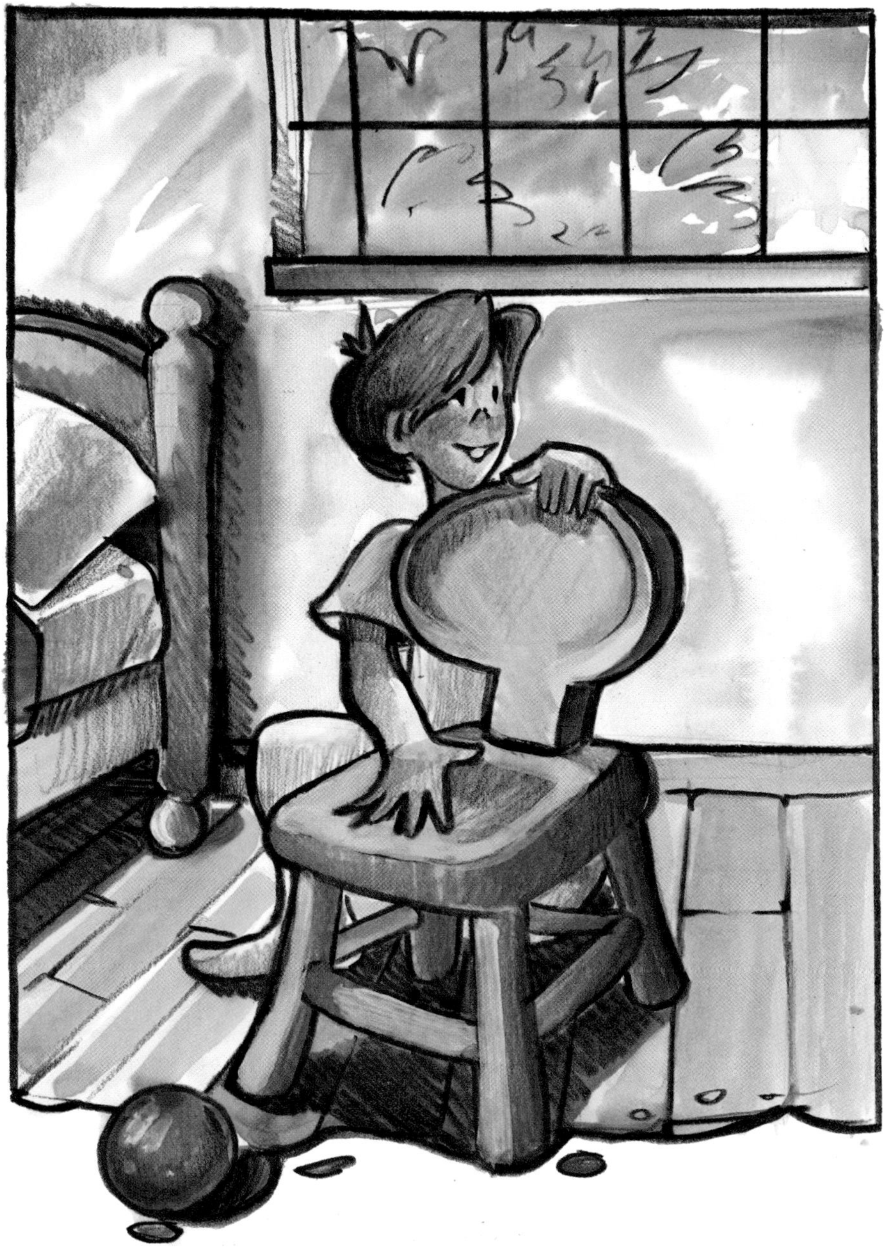

The chair is here.

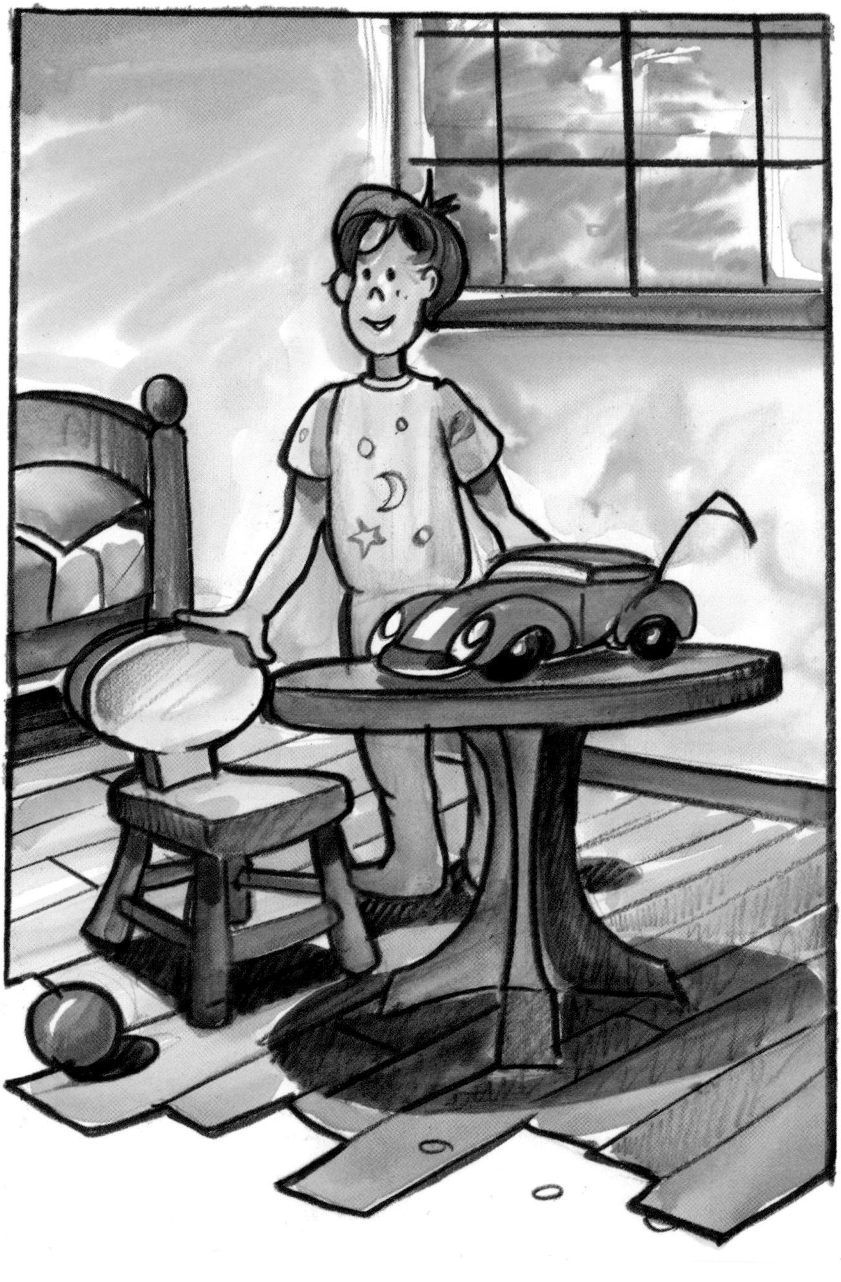

The table is here.

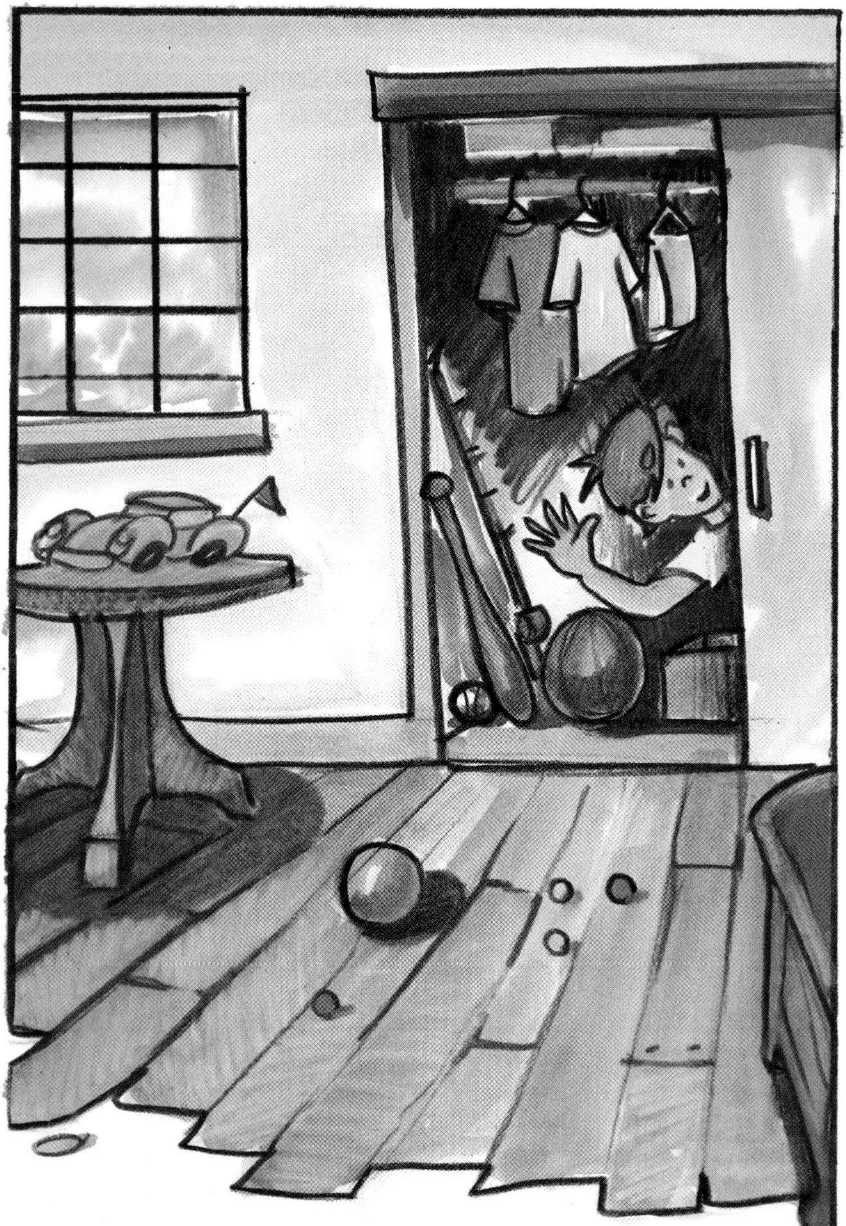

The closet is here.

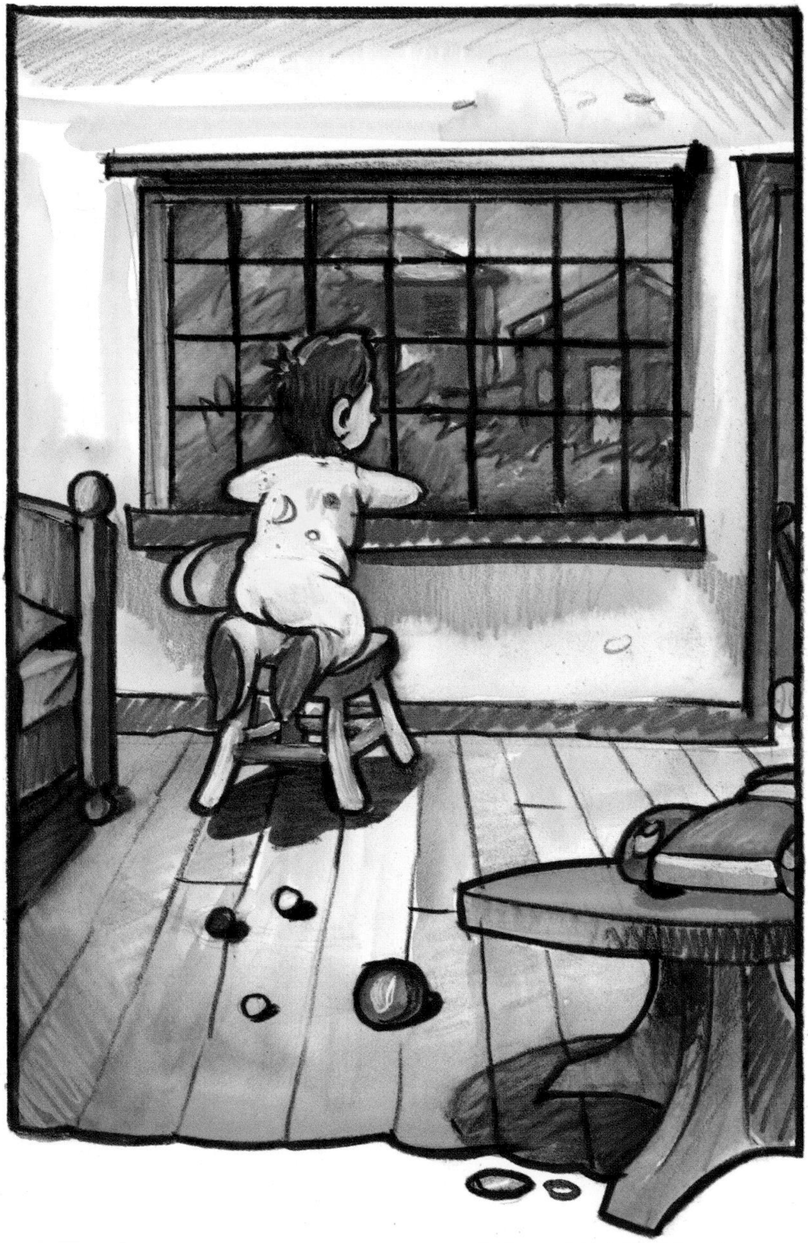

The window is here.

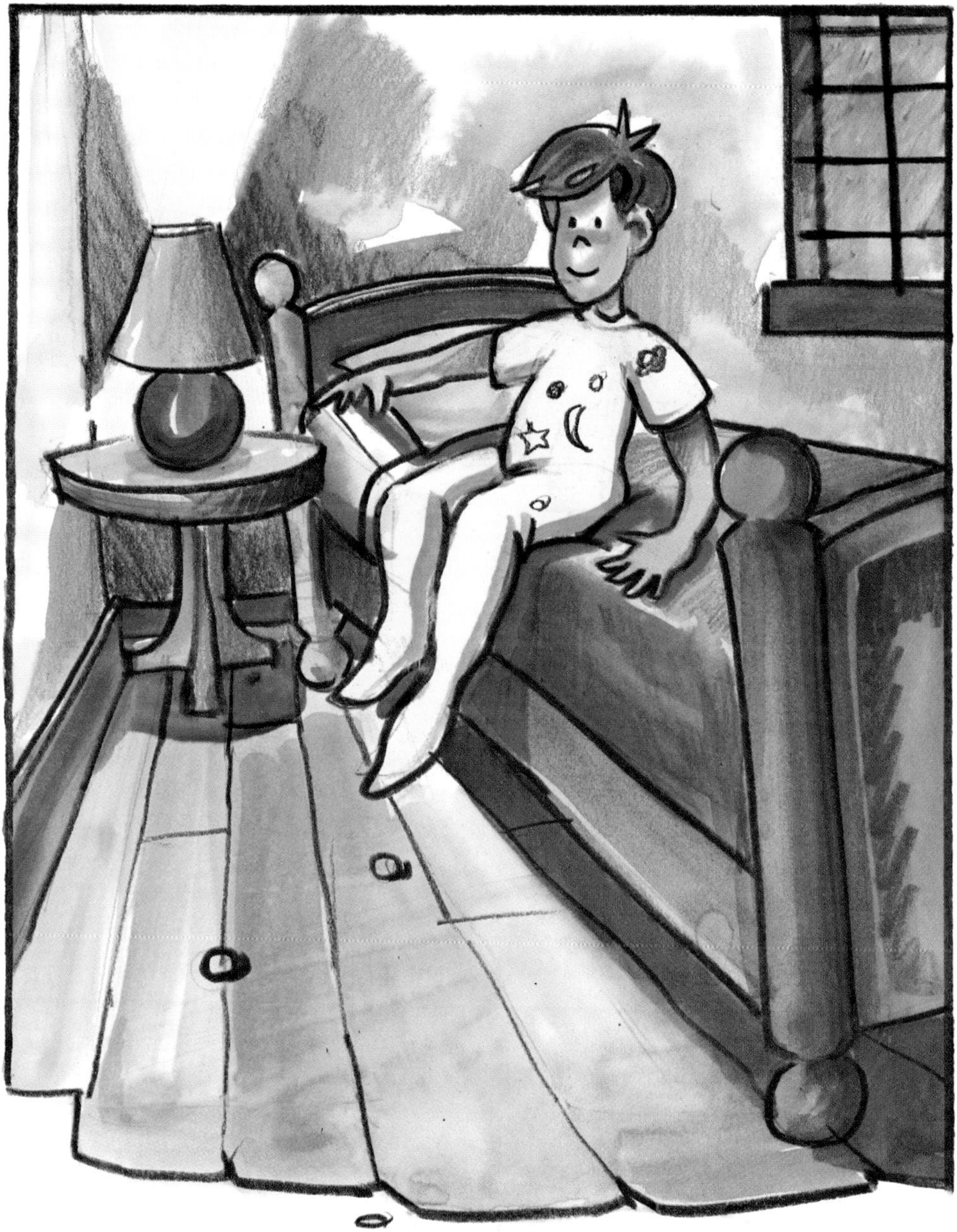

The light is here.

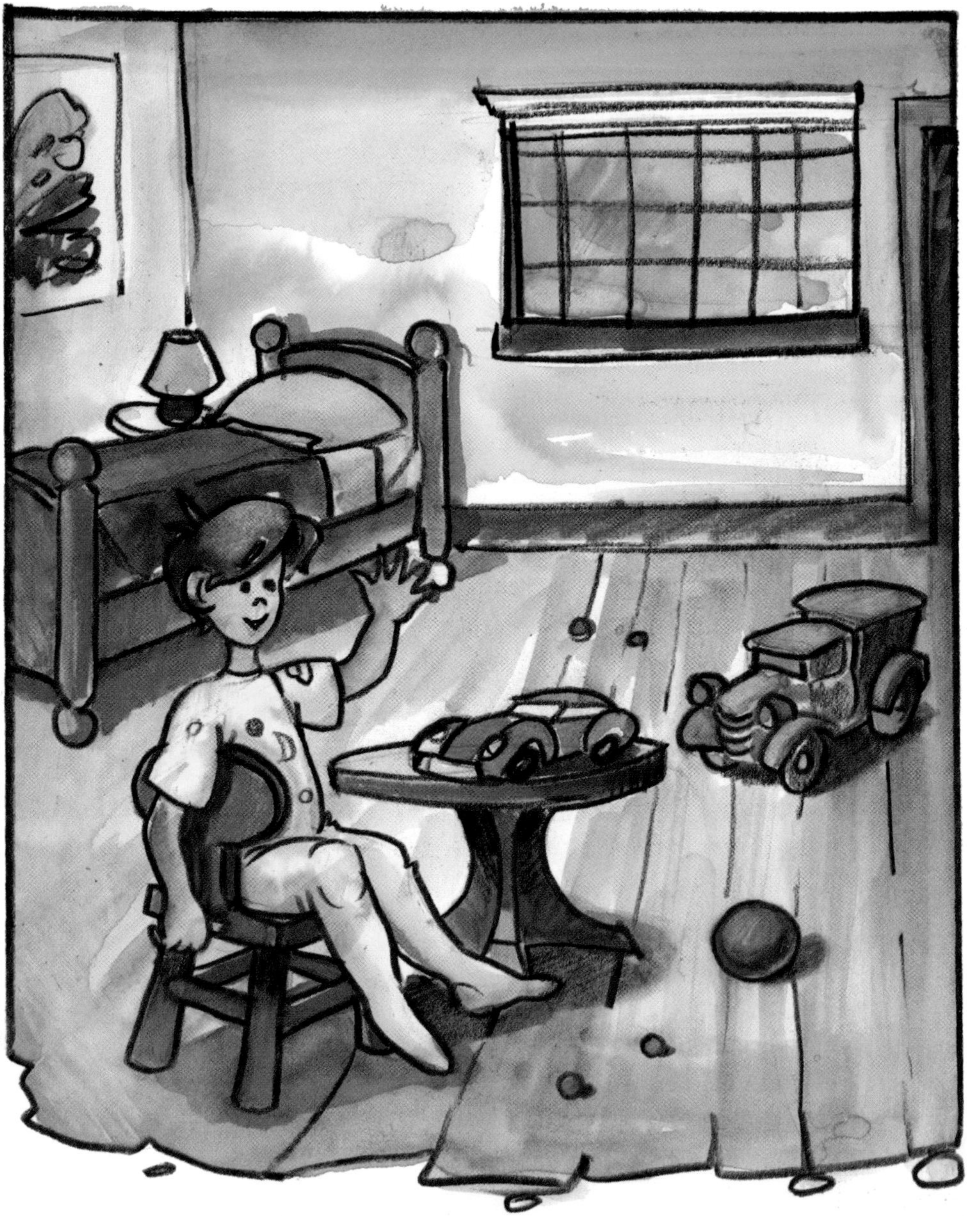

My room